From Austria to America: Franz Luger's Immigrant Experience

John C. Luger Jr.

I (John) would like to dedicate this book to the following individuals:

1. *Our family members, both alive and passed.*

2. *My Mother, Julie, my Wife, Family, and friends for all of the help and encouragement that they gave with this project.*

3. *Everyone who will read this book-You are making this very enjoyable for us all.*

4. *All of the immigrants to America.*

5. *The Lord, for allowing us life, what we have, and the abilities to write and publish this book.*

Table of Contents

Franz' Family

On May 29th, 1854, in House #8, in the town of Neustift Im Muehlkreis, in Upper Austria, in the *Austro-Hungarian Empire*, a baby was born to Mathias Luger and Anna Bogner.

They named him Francis Seraphim Luger. He would be known as 'Franz', eventually. He was the fifth of 9 children and was baptized in the parish church in a town known as Oberkappel, which is close by Neustift. His baptism record listed that his father, Mathias, was a *Haeusler*, or cottager, in German.

The Luger family was a middle class farming family that lived in and around Neustift for over two centuries. Mathias, his father, born in the area, and baptized in Oberkappel on February 21st, 1814, to Josef or Joseph Luger and Theresia Goettinger. He was a farmer, or in German, a *bauer*, just as his ancestors were.

Map of towns in Upper Austria
associated with the Luger Family.

On February 1st, 1847, Matthias married, in the *parish church* in Oberkappel, an Anna Bogner, who was born in May of 1818, in a neighboring town known as Pfarrkirchen Im Muehlkreis to a Blasius Bogner, a farmer and a Catharina Goettinger. They settled in the small village of Neustift, in House #8, and had a total of nine children:

1. Johann Nepomuk Luger, Baptized on May 16th, 1848
2. Karl Luger, Baptized on November 2nd, 1849
3. Josef Luger, Baptized on March 30th, 1851
4. Heinrich Luger, Baptized on July 7th, 1852
5. Franz Seraphim Luger, Baptized on May 29th, 1854

6. Leopold Luger, Baptized on August 5th, 1857
7. Maria Luger, Baptized on January 23rd, 1859
8. Rosa Luger, Baptized on August 9th, 1860
9. Katharina Luger, Baptized November 29th, 1861

Joseph Luger, Mathias' father, also a citizen of Neustift, was an *ausburger*, as listed on his death record. As an *ausburger*, he owned property outside of Neustift while being a citizen in that town and was a farmer as well. He was born in March of 1787, in Neustift, to Mathias Luger and his wife, Agnes Krenn. Theresia Goettinger was born in April of 1786, in a neighboring town named Aigen Im Muehlkreis to Matthias Goettinger and his wife, Elisabeth Loeffler.

Mathias Luger was born in a town, nearby Neustift, known as OberAschenburg, early in 1760 to Johann Luger and his wife Maria Anna Theresia Albenberger. He was baptized on February 22nd, 1760. Johann, according to the baptism record, was, in Latin, a *rustici*, probably a gentleman farmer. Matthias married Agnes Krenn in Neustift on February 3rd, 1785, the daughter of Mathias Krenn and his wife Anna Maria Grimbs. At the time of their marriage, the witnesses were Johann Luger, Mathias' father and Michael Krenn, Agnes' brother.

Matthias was also a farmer, as listed on his death record, as well.

Mathias' father, Johann Luger, was baptized in October of 1723, in a town in Bavaria, Germany, known as Passau, to Jacob Luger and Eva Haas.

Franz' Childhood

Franz and his family lived and grew up, in Neustift, in House #8. His childhood was the same as those of other children growing up in there, during the mid to late 1800's. When he was old enough, he went to the local village school, played with the other children in the village, and on Sundays, in the morning, he attended church services in the local *parish church* with his family.

In a typical Austrian village back then, life was routine for everyone living in it over the centuries. Franz's childhood consisted of helping around the household, going to the local school and learning the lessons being taught by the schoolmaster well. He was taught to respect his parents, relatives, and elders, taught to behave well and to stay out of trouble, and went to Church, on Sundays, with his family.

Upon reaching adolescence, his parents would select a trade for him to be *apprenticed* to, and when reaching adulthood, he would marry and start a family of his own. Franz would most likely have lived out his entire life in the village. He also would have died there and his family would have brought him to the church for the funeral service. After that, he would be buried in the local cemetery.

An Unhappy Event.

On March 26th, 1868, a terrible thing happened; his mother, Anna, died from *hepatitis*. It left Franz very upset and unhappy. Mathias remarried in 1871 to a lady named Franziska Bogner, and had more children with her. At about this time, in an endeavor to get his son set up and earning a living, and also wanting more for him than a job as a farmer, he had him *apprenticed* to a wagon maker. Franz would learn a trade and be able to earn money for himself and his family in the future.

Joining the Army

Even though his father provided for him and set him up with an occupation, Franz, because of the loss of his mother, still had an unhappy childhood. Probably, wanting to get away from the situation, as one reason, he decided to quit his job as a wagonmaker, join the *Austrian Emperor's* army, and start a new life and adventure for himself a long way away.

There was another reason why he enlisted into the army-he was required to do so by law. In 1867, the Emperor Franz Joseph decreed that there would be, from that point on, general *conscription* would be the law, in the *Austro-Hungarian Empire.* That meant that upon reaching the age of 18 years, every single male individual in the empire would automatically be required to serve in the army, whether peasant farmer or prince. Even paying for a substitute would not be allowed any longer.

Childhood Picture of Louis
Luger, Born in 1879.

There changes made in the *Austro-Hungarian military* and serving in it would have benefits, as the *Austro-Hungarian government* wanted to entice and inspire people to want to join the army. For example, the officer class would no longer be restricted to the *nobility*. This meant that individuals from the middle classes also could become officers as well, as the only requirement for being eligible was that they would be able to read, write, spell, figure, and understand general terms, instead of needing to be born into the royalty or *aristocracy*.

Also, cruel and unusual punishments in the military were abolished and if one completed their term of service successfully, they would have the opportunity to advance upwards, economically as well as socially, upon their release back into civilian life.

Childhood Picture of John Luger, Born in 1882.

Joining the army, Franz started out as a soldier, learned to march in formation, carry, use, and fire a rifle, keep his uniform clean, etc. Amongst his fellow soldiers, he, found friendship and a sense of belonging that he missed for a while. While watching how he performed, his superiors thought well of how he did and within time, Franz would be promoted to being an officer. He was finally happy!

During this time, Franz met someone named Franziska Baumgartner, who came from another town in Upper Austria known as Peilstein, and was the daughter of Jakob Baumgartner and Katharina Kasper. They had a son who they named Ludwig.

On January 7th, 1879, in Oberkappel, Franz was married to Anna Maria Eicker, who was born in about 1856 in Pfarrkirchen Im Muehlkreis, and was the daughter of Philip Eicker, a farmer, and Anna Maria Lang. Three years later, in December of 1882, their son, who they named Johann, or John, was born.

Picture of Franz Luger in Military Uniform and holding rifle, early 1880's.

Trouble

While things went well for him in the army, Franz got into trouble. He joined a political party that the Austrian Emperor did not like and the Austrian government learned of his involvement with the party. Because the Austrian Emperor did not like the idea of an army officer being part of a party that he didn't approve of, it meant serious consequences for Franz and his family, he was expelled from the army, and told to leave the *Austro-Hungarian Empire* and to take his family and possessions with him. In addition to this, his wife, Anna Maria Eicker died. Once again, a way of life that he knew and enjoyed was ruined!

Immigrating to America

Franz and his family did not have very long to be upset because of their terrible loss. The first thing that he had to figure out was how and where he would go and provide for himself and his family. They were not allowed to stay in the *Austro-Hungarian Empire* any longer. Even if they had been, things would not have been good for them. People who had been expelled the army were thought of and treated with scorn, and most likely, people would have considered it dangerous to associate with them.

Businesses would not employ him, landlords and landladies would not rent apartments to him and his family, stores would not serve him, and people would not want anything to do with him. His options in the Empire would have been limited, so the family needed to go and live somewhere far away where they wouldn't be so well-known and start life over again.

Fortunately, Franz and his family had some friends and relatives who told them about America, that large country on the other side of the world, where the streets were paved with gold.

If someone worked long and hard there, they would have a good life, and things would be much better for them than in the Empire. This was also a country, also, where people could choose their leaders in the form of voting for them, much different than what it was like in the Empire, and where they could speak their minds and not be in trouble with the government for it, where they could worship as they wanted to, instead of having their government decide that for them, and where they would not be deprived of life or liberty without due process of law, and much more!

In the end, the choice was easy for the Luger family to make, they would go to America and start their new life there!

Because the Luger family did not have enough money to make the long journey together, they realized that they would have to come to America separately. Franz needed to make the journey over, settle in a city, find employment, and save up money to bring the rest of the family over. The *Austro-Hungarian government* was

more concerned with getting him out quickly than the
rest of his family.

15

The Long Journey

Between late 1883 and early 1884, Franz bought his train and ship tickets, said goodbye to his family and friends, and boarded the train for the long journey. It would be ten years before he would have his family with him, and he would never see Austria again. He would not see his father Mathias, his stepmother Franziska, his brothers and sisters, or his stepbrothers and stepsisters again. Mathias died in 1897 in Neustift, without his son being with him.

While on the train trip to the port, Franz had lots of time to think about matters and did so: "Will I be able to build a good life in the new country?", "Will I be able to make a good living in the new country?", and "When will I see my family again?" among other thoughts.

Finally, the train arrived at the port in Hamburg, Germany, on March 30th, 1884. Franz boarded a ship called the *Lessing* and he left Europe forever from the port of La Havre in France. He started the long journey to America. During the journey, he had to ride in *steerage*, the area near the bottom of the ship.

Because they were almost at the bottom of the ship, traveling in *steerage* was not enjoyable for Franz and the other passengers. They were down there for most of the day, except for when the captain and crew allowed them to be on the deck for an hour or two. It was dark down there, the food, often, was poor, and the water, often, was stale. As well, the sanitation and hygiene of the passengers, sometimes, was poor. The passengers would have to live in these circumstances for the entire journey, which lasted weeks! Franz must have wondered if he'd survive the journey.

But he did survive it and on April 12th, 1884, he walked on the *gangplank* from the *Lessing* and went in to *Castle Garden*, a station for taking care of immigrants, with the others in New York City. He spent two weeks living in steerage, to be able to come to America.

Landing in America

Franz arrived in America at a time when there was a lot of controversy concerning immigrants and immigration. The topic was a dangerous subject. One group of people wanted to keep immigration going because, after all, America was a nation made from immigrants and they provided the country with the manpower that it needed to keep the it going and growing.

On the other side, several people did not want immigrants coming to the country. As far as they were concerned, some of the immigrants that came often had poor health and infectious diseases, their hygiene often was poor, if it existed at all, some had been in trouble with the law where they came from, and it was also feared that some would become public charges when they arrived and would need to be supported.

Also, *Castle Garden*, where Franz entered the country, was the subject of a lot of controversy! Originally, it was founded to provide immigrants with better circumstances then before. The station watched the newcomers, made sure that they were protected from dishonest individuals who wanted to steal their possessions, provided them with temporary shelters and meals, and gave them train tickets for their journey to wherever they wanted to go.

Before *Castle Garden* came into existence, immigrants were simply dropped off of the ship upon arrival and allowed to go their way. They often fell victim to thieves and other dishonest individuals who stole their possessions from them.

Although *Castle Garden* was set up with the best of intentions, trouble eventually started, and it included corrupt administrators and *immigrant runners*, people who defrauded the immigrants, getting too close to the newcomers, etc. Also, Castle Garden was only a state run operation that the United States Federal Government couldn't control or reform. About 6 years after Franz arrived, *Castle Garden* was closed down and a new station was opened up on *Ellis Island* that was operated by the United States Federal Government.

Settling in Saint Paul, Minnesota

While at *Castle Garden*, Franz had to decide where he would go to start a new life for himself and his family. For reasons that only he knew, he decided that it would be best to make that start in a city in the Midwest known as Saint Paul, in Minnesota, and purchased a train ticket to go there. For the first part of the journey, he traveled by rail from New York City to Chicago. When he arrived in Chicago, he boarded another train headed to Saint Paul. Because he didn't have much money, he had to buy a third class ticket and he sat and slept in a seat, watching everything that the train went by. He observed more of the new country and also listened to the blowing of the locomotive's steam whistle and the pounding of the wheels on the rails. By 1886, Franz was in Saint Paul and he needed to get settled down in the city. First, he had to find a job, and then he had to find a place to live.

Franz began walking through the city, looking into the windows of businesses for "Help Wanted" signs. He couldn't speak English and trying to understand what was being said was a major source of trouble. He was alone and didn't know anyone. Eventually, he encountered some Germans who were immigrants themselves, who told him about a wagonmaking company owned by two individuals known as *Brandl & Stiegelbauer.*

The owners felt some empathy towards the newly arrived Austrian immigrant, as they were German, and might have been immigrants themselves. In addition to this, they must have been happy to find out that he was a wagonmaker and his experience doing that would be a valuable asset to their company, so they hired him. Now that he had employment, Franz was able

to find a place to live and he was living in an apartment at 608 Lafond Street, in the city.

Over the next ten years, Franz changed occupations and residences several times and worked hard to save up money to bring his family to Minnesota. During this time, he also made transitions from the Austrian way of life to the American way of life. He learned that life in America was different than in Austria. For example, instead of being called 'Franz', as he was in Austria, he was called 'Frank', he found that the currency that he used in Austria had to be replaced with American currency. He had to learn what a dollar was, as well as a half-dollar, quarter, dime, nickel, and penny all were. He also had to learn that some of the customs and manners that were acceptable and expected in Austria were not allowed or expected in America. He found that German, his native language, was not expected and used as much in America, and that he needed to learn how to speak English, instead. There also were new customs and manners that he was expected to learn and practice, as well.

Learning to speak English was a lifelong struggle for Franz, and he often had to have friends and relatives communicate for him since he wasn't able to speak English easily.

Bringing the Rest of the Family Over

Franz had to work almost seven years, changing jobs and places to live several times, but by 1893 he saved up enough money to bring the rest family from Austria to Minnesota. A passenger list from a ship dating to June 24th, 1893, showed the last of his family, Franziska his wife, and Ludwig(Louis) their son, entering America at *Ellis Island.* John, his son by Anna Maria Eicker, arrived earlier.

Ludwig Luger,
Ca.1895.

By the end of 1893, the Luger family was living together in Saint Paul. On September 11th, 1893, in Saint Agnes' Parish, Franz and Franziska were married. In 1894, they welcomed another child into their family; a daughter who they named Anna. Their family was now complete.

Franz and Franziska Luger, 1890's.

After having worked at several jobs which didn't work out, Franz found a job that he enjoyed doing and was good at in the metal industry. The 1899 Saint Paul City Directory listed him as working as a *grinder* in a metalworking company. In 1900, the United States Federal Census noted that he was working as a *brass polisher* for the Union B & M Manufacturing Company in Saint Paul.

Franz and Franziska Luger and Family, Ca.1895.

Anna Luger, Born in 1894.

Later Years

As the 1900's became the 1910's, Franz and Franziska
saw their children grow up and make lives of their own.
Ludwig, the eldest, started out working as a *helper* in the
Saint Paul Brass Foundry. By 1910 he was tending and
maintaining the fires there. Back in 1910, in order to
heat up the metal, so
that it could be forged,
fire needed to be used.
It was his job to make
sure that the fires were
hot and intense
enough so that work
could be done and if
they weren't he had to
drop more coal and
other fuel in the fires

Metal Spinning Shop where
John Luger worked-
Ca.1910.

to get them to the right temperatures. He worked at
that job for several years. Also in 1910, he bought a

house for himself and his family on Thomas Street, in Saint Paul.

John started working between the ages of 17 & 18 at the brass foundry as *a metal spinner*, operating a lathe. Back in the early 20th century, when individuals wanted to do sculpting or detailing on metal, they used a machine called a *lathe*. A *lathe* consisted of a rotating apparatus that the metal was fastened to. The apparatus had a *pulley*, or rotating disk attached to it, belts were attached to the pulley and another pulley which was attached to a motor. When the motor was turned on, the *pulleys* that were attached it and the entire lathe turned, and the worker did whatever detailing and sculpting that needed to be done on the metal while it was turning.

2nd Picture of Metal Spinning Shop where John Luger worked-Ca.1910.

He worked as a *metal spinner* there until 1930, when he started his own metal spinning company. He was the first business owner in the Luger family in America!

Ludwig Luger and Marie Frank Wedding Picture, 1902

John and Bertha Luger & Bertha Luger-Ca.1905.

Anna, their daughter, also started working when she was a very young girl. This was the era of child labor. In 1909, between the ages of 14 & 15, she worked as a *spooler* in a textile mill. Two years later, in 1911, she was working as a *helper* there.

Between 1902 and the early 1910's, Franz and Franziska watched their children get married and start families of their own. Louis met Marie Frank, and they were married on August 19th, 1902. They had three children: James Louis, in 1903, Harold, in 1906, and Wallace, in 1914.

Bertha M. Klar's Family-Ca.1905

John met Bertha M. Klar, the daughter of Ferdinand Tyrok and Pauline Klar. Pauline Klar and her stepfather Frank Paschella lived close by in Saint Paul on Lafond Street with her younger stepbrother Frank Paschella Jr. In November of 1904, John and Bertha were married in Saint Agnes Parish in Saint Paul. They had three children, as well: Theodore, in 1905, Raymond, in 1911, and Helen, in 1916.

Franz and
Franziska Luger in
Later Years.

Theodore Luger,
Born in 1905.

Anna met and married Nicholas Strohmeyer, in the early 1910's and they had three children together: Louise, in 1915, Frank, in 1916, and Bernard John, in 1917. Frank Strohmeyer would be a best man for his cousin Raymond, at the time of his marriage to a lady named Margaret Rita Shea in 1938. Franz and Franziska got to enjoy being grandparents!

Franz continued working at the *brass foundry* as a *grinder* well into his later years. For him, it was a job that he was able to do well and must have liked.

During the last years of his life, Franz worked at the foundry to support Franziska and his family, resting more often, of course, and spending time with his grown up children and grandchildren.

Theodore Luger, Helen Luger, Born in 1916, and Ravmond.

On these occasions, he would tell his grandchildren about growing up in Austria and what it was like to come to America and start a new life there. When his grandson Raymond asked him about it, he attempted to share the stories with them.

Helen Luger, Born in 1916.

Theodore Luger and Theodore Luger and
Raymond Luger, Born in 1911.

Death

At is usually happens in life, Franz' health declined in his later years. He had worked long hours in the *foundry* and eventually wasn't able to cope with the rigors and demands of life any longer. He went to Bethesda Hospital in Saint Paul for treatment and died there on February 3rd, 1931.

After his funeral, he was buried in Calvary Cemetery in Saint Paul. He lived a long and full life, worked hard, took care of, raised, and provided for his family. He wouldn't be forgotten by them or anyone else who knew him. Franz Luger would be known by many for having been successful as an immigrant who came to America and started a new life there!

Franz Luger's Family Tree

Generation 1.

1. Franz Seraphim Luger

Born in May of 1854, in Neustift im Muehlkreis, Upper Austria, Austria. Baptized on May 29th, 1854, in Oberkappel, Upper Austria, Austria. Died on February 3rd, 1931, Saint Paul, Ramsey County, Minnesota

Generation 2.

1. Matthias Luger

Born on February 21st, 1814, in Oberkappel, Upper Austria, Austria. Died in 1897, in Neustift Im Muehlkreis, Upper Austria Austria. Married on February 1st, 1847, in Oberkappel, Upper Austria, Austria

2. Anna Bogner

Born in May of 1818, in Pfarrkirchen, Upper Austria, Austria. Died on March 26th, 1868, in Neustift Im Muehlkreis, Upper Austria, Austria

Child was Franz Seraphim Luger

Born in May of 1854, in Neustift im Muehlkreis, Upper Austria, Austria

Generation 3.

1. Josef (Joseph) Luger

Baptized on March 13th, 1787, in Neustift Im Muehlkreis, Upper Austria, Austria. Died in 1861, Neustift Im Muehlkreis, Upper Austria, Austria.

2. Theresia Goettinger

Baptized on June 9th, 1786, in Aigen im Muehlkreis, Upper Austria, Austria. Died Before 1816, Probably in Upper Austria, Austria.

Child was Matthias Luger

Born on February 21st, 1814, Oberkappel, Upper Austria, Austria.

3. Blasius Bogner

Born in About 1778, in Upper Austria, Austria.

4. Catharina(Catherine) Goettinger

Born in About 1783, in Upper Austria Austria.

Child was Anna Bogner

Born in May of 1818, in Pfarrkirchen, Upper Austria, Austria.

Generation 4.

1.   Mathias Luger

Born in February of 1760, Probably in OberAschenberg, Upper Austria, Austria. Died in 1812, Neustift Im Muehlkreis, Upper Austria, Austria. Married in 1785, in Neustift Im Muehlkreis, Upper Austria, Austria.

2.   Agnes Kren or Krenn

Born Before 1765, Probably in Upper Austria, Austria.

Child was Josef Luger

Baptized on March 13th, 1787, in Neustift Im Muehlkreis, Upper Austria, Austria.

3.   Matthias Goettinger

Born Before 1751, Probably in Upper Austria, Austria.

4.   Elisabeth Loeffler

Born Before 1751, Probably in Upper Austria, Austria.

Child was Theresia Goettinger

Baptized June 9th, 1786, in Aigen Im Muehlkreis, Upper Austria, Austria.

5.   Leopold Bogner

Born Before 1753, Probably in Upper Austria, Austria.

6.   Rosina Buchmayer

Born February 5th, 1732, in Windhaag Per Haag, Upper Austria, Austria.

Child was Blasius Bogner

Born in About 1778, in Upper Austria, Austria.

7.   Leonhard Goettinger

Born Before 1742, in Upper Austria, Austria.

8.   Elisabeth Gattinger

Born Before 1763, in Upper Austria, Austria.

Child was Catharina Goettinger

Born in About 1783, in Upper Austria, Austria.

Generation 5.

1.   Johann Luger

2.   Maria Anna Theresia Albenberger

Children was Matthias Luger

Born in February 1760, Probably in OberAschenberg, Upper Austria, Austria.

3.   Mathias Krenn

4.   Anna Maria Grimbs

Child was Agnes Krenn

Born Before 1765, Probably in Upper Austria, Austria.

5.   Gregory Goettinger

6.   Anna Maria Parthin or Parth

Child was Matthias Goettinger

Born Before 1751, Probably in Upper Austria, Austria.

7.   Dominic Loefler

8.   Magdalena Staibher

Child was Elisabetha Loeffler

Born Before 1751, Probably in Upper Austria, Austria.

9.   Johann Bogner

10.   Catharina(Catherine)

Child was Leopold Bogner

Born Before 1753, Probably in Upper Austria, Austria.

11.   Michael Buchmayer

12.   Katharina Panhofer

Child was Rosina Buchmayer

Baptized on February 5th, 1732, in Windhaag Bei Perg, Upper Austria, Austria.

13.   Christopher Gattinger

14.   Susanna

Child was Leonard Gattinger

Born Before 1742, Probably in Upper Austria, Austria.

15.   Mathias Gattinger

16.   Sabina Sophia Schaechlinger

Children were:

1.   Catharina Gattinger

Born Before 1763, Probably in Upper Austria, Austria.

2.   Jakob Gattinger

Born in About 1770, Probably in Upper Austria, Austria. Married October 27th, 1794, in Voecklabruck, Upper Austria, Austria

17. Katharian Dietl

Bibliography

1. Luger Family, Questions and Answers, 1984 to Present Day, Minnesota

2. "Hamburg Passenger Lists, 1850-1934 for Franz Luger",

Ancestry.com(http://interactive.ancestryinstitution.com/:Accessed 15Apr2014)

3."Hamburg Passenger Lists, 1850-1934 about Franz Luger",

Ancestry.com(http://search.ancestryinstitution.com/:Accessed 15Apr2014)

4. "Mathias Luger in the Upper Austria, Austria, Catholic Church Registers, 1614-1938",

Ancestry.com(http://ancestry.com/discoveryui-content/view/:Accessed 11Jan2023)

5."Franz Luger in the Upper Austria, Austria, Catholic Church Registers, 1614-1938",

Ancestry.com(http://ancestry.com/discoveryui-content/view/:Accessed 11Jan2023)

6."Joseph Luger in the Upper Austria, Austria, Catholic Church Registers, 1614-1938",

Ancestry.com(http://ancestry.com/discoveryui-content/view/:Accessed 11Jan2023)

7."Joseph Lueger in the Upper Austria, Austria, Catholic Church Registers, 1614-1938",

Ancestry.com(http://ancestry.com/discoveryui-content/view/:Accessed 11Jan2023)

8."Matthias Luger in the Upper Austria, Austria, Catholic Church Registers, 1614-1938",

 Ancestry.com(http://ancestry.com/discoveryui-content/view/:Accessed 11Jan2023)

9."Theresia Gottinger in the Upper Austria, Austria, Catholic Church Registers, 1614-1938",

 Ancestry.com(http://ancestry.com/discoveryui-content/view/:Accessed 11Jan2023)

10."Blasius Bogner in the Upper Austria, Austria, Catholic Church Registers, 1614-1938",

 Ancestry.com(http://ancestry.com/discoveryui-content/view/:Accessed 12Jan2023)

11.Peter Lemke, "Familie Krenner"

 Ancestry.com(https://ancestry.com/family-tree/person/tree/:Accessed 13Jan2023)

12."Matthias Goettinger in the Upper Austria, Austria, Catholic Church Registers, 1614-1938",

 Ancestry.com(http://ancestry.com/discoveryui-content/view/:Accesed 13Jan2023)

13."Leopold Bogner in the Upper Austria, Austria, Catholic Church Registers, 1614-1938",

 Ancestry.com(http://ancestry.com/discoveryui-content/view/:Accessed 13Jan2023)

14."Leonard Gottinger in the Upper Austria, Austria, Catholic Church Registers, 1614-1938",

 Ancestry.com(http://ancestry.com/discoveryui-content/view/:Accessed 15Jan2023)

15."H Gregor Gottinger in the Upper Austria, Austria, Catholic Church Registers, 1614-1938",

Ancestry.com(http://ancestry.com/discoveryui-content/view/:Accessed 15Jan2023)

16."Dominicus Loeffler in the Upper Austria, Austria, Catholic Church Registers, 1614-1938",

Ancestry.com(http://ancestry.com/discoveryui-content/view/:Accessed 17Jan2023)

17."Joannes Bogner in the Upper Austria, Austria, Catholic Church Registers, 1614-1938",

Ancestry.com(http://ancestry.com/discoveryui-content/view/:Accessed 17Jan2023)

18."Catharina Goettinger in the Upper Austria, Austria, Catholic Church Registers, 1614-1938",

Ancestry.com(http://ancestry.com/discoveryui-content/view/:Accessed 21Jan2023)

19."Blasius Bogner in the Upper Austria, Austria, Catholic Church Registers, 1614-1938",

Ancestry.com(http://ancestry.com/discoveryui-content/view/:Accessed 25Jan2023)

20.Anja Kirchbaumer, "Baumgartner-Leitner 20...",

Ancestry.com(https://ancestry.com/family-tree/person/tree/:Accessed 25Jan2023)

21."Matthias Gattinger in the Upper Austria, Austria, Catholic Church Registers, 1614-1938",

Ancestry.com(http://ancestry.com/discoveryui-content/view/:Accessed 27Jan2023)

22."Mathias Gattinger in the Upper Austria, Austria, Catholic Church Registers, 1614-1938",

Ancestry.com(http://ancestry.com/discoveryui-content/view/:Accessed 27Jan2023)

23."Mathias Luger in the Upper Austria, Austria, Catholic Church Registers, 1614-1938",

 Ancestry.com(http://:ancestry.com/discoveryui-content/view/:Accessed 27Jan2023)

24.Parish of Saint Agnes, "Luger Baumgartner Marriage Record", 11Sep1893,

 p.46, Diocese of Saint Paul-Minneapolis, Saint Paul, Minnesota

25.Matricula(http://data.matricula-online/eu/en/oesterreich/oberoesterreich/oberkappel/:

 Accessed 11Oct2023)

26.Matricula(http://data.matricula-online/eu/en/oesterreich/oberoesterreich/oberkappel/:

 Accessed 17Oct2023)

27."Leberentzendueng",

Collins Dictionary

(http://collinsdictionary.com/us/dictionary/german-english/leberentzendung/:

 Accessed 11Dec2023)

28."Hausler Family History",

 Ancestry.com(http://ancestry.com/:Accessed 11Dec2023)

29.John C. Luger Jr, "Ancestors of the Luger Family Volume No.1"

 Published Between 1999-2023, Forest Lake, Minnesota

30.Vincent J. Cannato, "American Passage, The History of Ellis Island",

 2009, Harper Collins Publishers, New York, New York

Acknowledgement

My Wife, Julie and My Mother.
All of our Family and Friends who helped and encouraged with this book.
The Lord.

About the Author

John Luger has always been interested in history and genealogy since childhood. Along with his wife, Julie, he also co-owns a genealogy research business named Family History Hunter. John and Julie both believe that the impact of immigration on America and American families is one that should always receive attention and appreciation. They also believe that immigration and history are topics youngsters should know about. It is their hope that through reading this book, they will start to develop an interest in these topics.